LAST POEMS

THOMAS KINSELLA was born in Dublin in 1928. He attended University College Dublin, entering the Civil Service before becoming a full-time writer and teacher in the United States. He was the author of over thirty collections of poetry, and translated extensively from the Irish, notably the great epic *The Táin*. He was a director of the Dolmen Press and Cuala Press, Dublin, and in 1972 founded Peppercanister Press for the publication of sequences and long and occasional poems. The editor of *The New Oxford Book of Irish Verse* and of Austin Clarke's *Selected Poems* and *Collected Poems*, Thomas Kinsella was also the author of *The Dual Tradition* (Carcanet), a critical essay on poetry and politics in Ireland. His awards and honours included Guggenheim Fellowships, the Denis Devlin Memorial Award, the Irish Arts Council Triennial Book Award and honorary doctorates from the University of Turin and the National University of Ireland. In 2007 Thomas Kinsella was awarded the Freedom of the City of Dublin. He died in December 2021.

also by
THOMAS KINSELLA
from Carcanet

Butcher's Dozen
Late Poems
Fat Master
Love Joy Peace
Prose Occasions
Selected Poems
Marginal Economy
Readings in Poetry
Collected Poems
Citizen of the World
Littlebody
Godhead
The Familiar
From Centre City
The Pen Shop
The Dual Tradition

Last Poems

Thomas Kinsella

CARCANET POETRY

First published in Great Britain in 2023 by
Carcanet
Alliance House, 30 Cross Street
Manchester, M2 7AQ
www.carcanet.co.uk

A CIP catalogue record for this book is
available from the British Library.

ISBN 978 1 80017 335 4

Book design by Andrew Latimer
Printed in Great Britain by SRP Ltd, Exeter, Devon

The publisher acknowledges financial
assistance from Arts Council England.

CONTENTS

LAST POEMS

'Where nature simply made, you understand.'
    Michelangelo, Sonnet XI: to Giorgio Vasari

MARGINAL ECONOMY

Wandering alone
from abandoned room to room
down the corridors of a derelict hotel,
searching for the lost urinal...

I woke,
        breathing a mental smell,
and tasted the night facts.

Nightwomen,
picking the works of my days apart,
will you find what you need
in the waste still to come?

FIRST NIGHT

The older people in the neighbourhood
knew him and stayed clear.
Before they found themselves
laid hold of again, up against the counter.

Talking in his corner about the early days,
and the way everything went wrong. Refusing to take in
the realities of the past forty years;
the long sentences finding their way
to a legalistic close.

                    But there was no one else left
who had known all the major figures.
And I had learned to stand near
in case there was something he hadn't said before.
And sometimes there was someone new starting to listen.
As I was, that first night.

                    I had moved in
to the flat across the street: a naked room
up under the roof, with a thin bed;
the widows' voices calling across the landing below.

And taken my first look in the dead moonlight
across the old roofs, back toward the edge of the city,
the new slum I had just left
– her teeth and glasses distinct on the night street.
Our voices unforgiving, exchanging refusals.

My brain at the window,
absorbing a new view of the world.
City loneliness.
One footstep down at the corner.

I saw the lights of the bar opposite,
checked I had enough left for a drink

... and was counting out the change, and turning away,
when I felt his presence beside me at the counter
on his high stool, his back against the partition.

After a few remarks, exchanged as though
I had been gone only a while,
                              he started talking.

THE AFFAIR

Standing, watching, on opposite sides of the grave,
we exchanged nods in old dislike.

*

Our affair. How it began…

At a Government inquiry in the early Fifties,
finding ourselves placed together;
our perfunctory talk growing rapidly watchful.

My picking on one of his self-admiring tropes.
His fastening on something slack of mine in return.
A raw wound opening on the matter
of Yeats and Fascism. A lasting animus
established in less than quarter of an hour.

Aware from then on.
                                    Our careers unrelated
but touching. Even in their beginnings:
in the same section, in the same Department;
his thought processes – his initials like insects –
earlier all over my files.

Recently, and sharpening our exchange
across the grave, his finding the occasion
in the press of public affairs
– debating his fixed viewpoints
in a three-piece colonial accent –

for an acid review: a flow of colloquialisms
dismissing a main thesis to be found
only in a misreading of the images off the cover…

*

The coffin touched bottom
with our gentle friend.
Goldenhaired. Spent in the service.

The prayers faded on the air.
The diggers stepped forward
to their pile by the open hole,
their hands around their shovels.

It was time for us to go
– his thick back moving off
familiar among the others.

WEDDING SERVICE

We approached the College chapel
along a gravel path by the old Library,
and across a wide private square in the heart of the City.

There was no trouble parking the car.
Once the scrutiny is over at the back gate
you are in a protected world:

the car door shut, and the sound
died along an avenue of old trees.

A quiet walk, past a park and playing fields.
Across the square to the chapel porch,
where the bridegroom received us, kindly and tall.

Full of care for her guests, he showed us in
– those of us liable to be unfamiliar –
all the way to our places
in an enclosed pew, on a low seat.

                          *

I looked about me.
At the plain walls panelled in ancient wood.
The pulpit out in the middle of the floor.
The aisle windows rising with plain glass
to the timbered ceiling.
Three coloured windows at the far end
above an empty platform.
                                    With a tang in the air.
Asiatic; familiar and out of place.

The other ill-fitting particulars
ourselves, settling down, over-aware,
where we sat. Looking across
at a number of other guests. Looking at us.

Soon the families and the more immediate guests
had assembled and walked in procession
between us to their places.

*

Out of sight, a little bell rang.
A priest entered, with a single server,
carrying between them
the tabernacle, the chalice and the Book;
a censer, tossing and exhaling.
Everything needed for the Mass

in this place purged of sacrifice
and the recognition of our dark side.
No murmuring over body and blood.

And Mass was said; diffident and determined.
With a brief address after the Communion
for the special occasion
– spiced with a few remarks for its happening here.

After which the celebrant stepped forward
to the waiting couple, and raised his right hand
in the coloured light, to bear witness.

The Bride comely.
The Groom steadfast.
Their hands primal

The ring fixed on her thin finger
in lovingkindness
and firm succession of the flesh.

BLOOD OF THE INNOCENT

I

From the day she was discovered
we watched over her and gave in to her,
and let her have everything.

But kept her to herself.
She grew lonely and sunk in on herself,
yawning in everybody's face.

*

We are gathered in rows
          on the steep steps,
a single being
          breathing together.

He stands at the block
          in the place of praise,
with apron stiff
          and jewelled beard.

II

The last time in anybody's memory
there was anything like this up here
was when that young local genius
tried to get them to change the system,

persuading the Authorities
that making an offering back to the source
with an act of thanks
is an interruption of the process.

That the life-form as we have it
is inadequate in itself; but that
having discovered the compensatory devices

of Love and the creative and religious imaginations
we should gather in each generation
all the good we can from the past,

add our own best and,
advancing in our turn
                              outward into the dark,

leave to those behind us,
with Acts of Hope and Encouragement,
a growing total of Good (adequately recorded),

the Arts and the Sciences,
with their abstractions and techniques
– all of positive human endeavour –

in a flexible and elaborating
time-resisting fabric
of practical and moral beauty...

                    *

Meek and mild
       with body marked,
our dear daughter
       steps forward.

MARCUS AURELIUS

I *On the Ego*

Gaspbegotten. In shockfuss.
          Out of nowhere.

Bent in blind sleep
          over a closed book.

Through the red neck
          cast out,

his first witness
          the gasp of loss,

to lie spent a while
          in the bloodstained shallows.

A little flesh. A little breath.
          And the mind governing.

Affairs were trouble in those days,
with over-confidence and ignorance everywhere.
A citizen, absent a while on an undertaking,
would find only increased coarseness on his return.

He himself, notable in his time and place,
and a major figure as later times would agree
(though for reasons that would have surprised his fellow citizens)
was in a false position:

                    cast in a main role,
while fitted with the instincts of an observer;
contending throughout his life with violent forces
that were to him mainly irrelevant.

Threatened on the Northern border by brutal tribes
with no settled homes – swift in the attack,
inspiring great fear; but ignorant and unskilled,
swift equally in the retreat –

these he dealt with, stemming their advance
and scattering them among their own confusions.
It was after his death that they resumed their incursions
that led to the break-up of the Western Empire.

A vaguer-seeming contagion out of the East,
more decisive in the longer term – in the citizens'
depths of will, and their dealings among themselves –
this he neglected.

                    Though it seems in retrospect

that nothing of any substance could have been done.
That it was irresistible
and in the movement and nature of things.

Called upon for decisive positive action,
at which he was more than averagely effective;
but preferring to spend his time in abstract inquiry,
for which he was essentially ungifted;

he kept a private journal, in Greek, for which
he is best remembered. Almost certainly
because it engaged so much of the baffled humane
in him, in his Imperial predicament:

accepting established notions of a cosmos
created and governed by a divine intelligence
– while not believing in an afterlife;

proposing exacting moral goals, with man
an element in that divine intelligence
– while pausing frequently to contemplate

the transient brutishness of earthly life,
our best experience of which concludes
with death, unaccountable and blank.

As to the early Christians, who might have helped
with their simplicities, he took no interest,
unsystematic in their persecution,
permitting their martyrdoms to run their course.

III

Faustina, wife of Marcus, developed a passion
for a certain gladiator. She confessed this
to her husband, who had the gladiator killed
and his wife bathed in the blood. They lay together,
and she conceived and brought into the world
the son Commodus, who grew to rule – with Marcus,
and as sole ruler after Marcus' death;
coming to terms quickly with the Northern tribes.

His rule was arbitrary, bloody-minded,
centred on the Games; and culminated
in the belief that he was Hercules.
His plan to appear for an Imperial function
in the arena, dressed as a gladiator,
led to public outcry, and his assassination,
strangled in private among his close advisers.
His death, succeeded by chaos and civil war,
ended one of the Empire's longest periods
of civic affluence and stability.

SONGS OF EXILE

I

In dust of the desert
Your tired tribe
awaited the word

– the first fathers
debating together
which would occasion
Your greater pain:

fade and exit
pure and faithful,
or soiled survival
dispersed on the world;

the first mothers
with low voices
and parts pursed
beside the fire.

*

The women grouped
in the rear gallery;
the male chorus
calling together

– women veiled
without a word;
men's mouths
wide open;

a sterile solo
    rising up,
the song ascending
    blank in gender
pale and professional
    up to the Father.

In soiled survival,
awaiting the Word,
we are here assembled.

II

We were a closed community.
The young ones wore their sex tight
in a slum without rest;
    revelling in noise and gang,
    spitting irresponsible.

The soul confined,
    her face pressed against the lattice.
Looking out at the day and the bright details
    descending, selecting themselves
    and settling in their own light.

MARGINAL ECONOMY

We worked farther out toward the edge
while anything could still be found.
Bringing back less and less,
until it was time to move again.
The need for care increasing.

We accepted things as they were,
with no thought of change.
The only change was in ourselves:
moving onward, leaving
something more behind each time.

There were ten years at most
even in the good places.

SONGS OF UNDERSTANDING

I

A major element of waste
  needed in the living process,
with an element of excess
  in the constituent materials;
distinguishing basic features
  performing no apparent function,
and playing no discernible part
  in countering any negative forces,
but which, if removed, would establish
  an emptiness under the heart.

I feel these, and allow my arms
  to fall open in resignation,
desiring an understanding.

II

Accepting the waste and the excess,
  and a fundamental inadequacy
in the structure as a whole
  and in each individual part,
there is still an ongoing dynamic
  in the parts as they succeed each other,
and in the assembling record,
  that registers as positive.

This can be thought of as purposeful,
  permitting the illusion,
to a self-selected few,
  of the positive participation

in a communal endeavour
  with a final meaningful goal
– imprecisely defined,
  subject to continual change

and calling for constant effort,
  but sufficient to give the feeling
of advancement toward an End.

III

Accepting out of the past
  The gift of the offered good,
add all of thine own best
  and offer the Gift onward.

IV

Through a fault on the outermost rim
  left open for the length of a lifetime
a glimpse of preoccupied purpose
  chilled the blood in my face.

RHETORIC OF NATURAL BEAUTY

A crimson ocean sunset
halved on a calm horizon

paused in seeming fullness
before the dark embrace.

In the face of God's creation
our last doubts fall silent,

fulfilled in acceptance,
reflect, and disappear.

MAN OF WAR

On being asked to sign
an appeal for the abolition of war

An epistle
to the hopeful in heart

ARGUMENT

A brutal basis in the human species,
native to man as beast, we must accept;
indifferent cruelty – a lack of pity –
in dealing with the lesser forms of life:
enjoyment in the hunt; the same enacted
in certain sports; an oral satisfaction
in chewing and savouring and swallowing
the slaughtered flesh.

                And there are forms of violence
sanctioned, or required, within the group
among aggressive males – in ordered strife
for mate, terrain or power; the choice established,
peace established while the victor rules.

But there is a mark not shared with the dumb beast:
the willed, and mass, occasional destruction
of others, face to face, of the same kind.   1

The spectacle of other living creatures
however fierce in slaughtering their quarry
or savaging their rivals for control,

organised for self-extermination
– employing every means at their disposal
and draining their essential life resources

to the detriment of every other need,
with prodigies of gallantry and skill
beyond exhaustion, reason or despair –

would startle and arrest. A just Observer
would choose to intervene, and save,

                    descending

with words of guidance: Mercy. Love. Control.   2
Inscribed on stone for permanence. If these
were disregarded... On to another world.

Onto the given world
                    the chosen species
emerged from the Garden with the mark upon them,

witnessed in their waste, and their first tracings
– flint blades in ashes, baby swords inserted
in toy bodies warring across the walls.

Diversified; increased across the earth,
hunting and gathering; worked the first soil
from rural settlements, semi-permanent;

discovered more of their profound potential
in static written cultures, under systems
of ordered conduct and agreed control

– even only as a shared ideal.
Evolved, from individual inspirations,
the principles of science, art and law.

Each aspect of the real, as discovered,
no sooner understood but put to use
in sharpening the instruments of war.

WAR

A conflict of significant duration,
significant but varying severity,
between contending comparable forces,
for varying objectives...

There are theorists,
studying the urge for self-destruction,
who still can find a meaningful connection
with animal, or natural, behaviour.

Others – for its absolute attrition,
methodical, determined and prolonged –
deny it any basis in the reason:
expressing a proclivity, obscure,
innate, toward negativity and loss.

The questioning continues, and the waste.   3

RETROSPECT

There was a certain grandeur in the past,
when ranks of the brave, in formal uniforms,
attacked each other in a place appointed,
and by agreement, on a chosen day.
Often after one side or the other
had marched for days through enemy terrain
enduring, and inflicting, fearful hardship.
And, while still exhausted, parched and hungry,
with no complaint, upon a certain signal,
advanced in formal groups against each other
with various kinds of deadly instruments
– sometimes on horseback, looking picturesque –
observing fixed conventions of behaviour
until the first shock of body contact.

Then the reality, the raw disorder
– discipline and breeding to the winds:
howling and rioting in all directions;
spears and rapiers into breasts and bowels;
axes hacking heads and necks asunder;
swords and sabres slicing arms and faces;
blades and barbs buried in body parts.

With cavalry involved, the cavalcade
– while adding extra colour to the chaos –
would have no meaning for the animals
lost in the bedlam: legs in disarray,
blood and entrails, heads flung up, jaws open,
whinnying and staring like mad fruit.

With arms evolving, and maturer methods,
wounds could be inflicted from a distance
– losing in control, unless the user
increased in skill; but gaining in effect:
a javelin could penetrate a body
and pin it to the ground; the bow and arrow,
restoring the precision while maintaining
the choice of range, offered a choice of use:
selectively, against a single target,
or copiously in shining showers of death.

*

These specialist, part-orderly excesses
of mutual self-slaughter would endure
the whole day, into the late evening,
ending in inertia and collapse,
with hosts of those engaged on either side
dead or dying, and the main survivors
useless for the balance of their lives
– maimed or blind or shocked out of their minds.

Then one side would surrender to the other
with matching acts of triumph and defeat:
the honourable sword of one commander
presented, humbly bowing, and accepted,
graciously indifferent, by the other.
Neither, very likely, having fought;
each holding to the remnants of convention,
speaking of future friendship – even honour,
though every rule of honour had been broken
while marching to the fray: the countryside
laid waste, cathedrals sacked and homes destroyed,
mothers raped and children massacred,
almost as an easement by the way.

Longer-term procedures were concluded
later, with a formal sealed agreement
recording terms in detail, and enshrining
humiliation of the beaten party,
with sacrificial bloodshed on occasion,
real or emblematic: leaders exiled,
hanged in public, or decapitated.

                            *

Peace with renewal. And equality
for the lower orders.
                            Self-annihilation
a given still, and occupying still
the same proportion of the human purpose,
the craft of warfare opened its embrace
to the base-born, excluded until now
or butchered by the way.
                            Allowed at last
an equal role in serious affairs,
the humble multitudes were drilled – skilled –
in dull disorder, uniform and drab,
to slay each other over the long term.

                            *

Organic balance…
                            As the splendour faded
the slaughter gained in deadliness and range.

Man gained in power and knowledge:

                                            from great heights
marauding fleets, selecting points of light,

leave behind them as they turn for home
each others' homes consumed.

                                        Matter and Man
melt in climax: satisfied, from on high,
a raping angel with a playful name
wipes his wings above a bowl of flame.

A PROPOSAL

It bothers me how simple it might be
to end the slaughter of the innocent
and reach the diplomatic stage direct.

In oral warfare: arguing the issues,
serious, in a game of verbal chess;
the loser underwriting the result
with his own life, in form and in the flesh.

But it seems the whole process is required;
the waste of lives, occasional, complete;
a purging, cleansing and calamitous;

lives of the young, chosen by circumstance
for purposes not theirs to understand.
For sacrifice.

*

        Accepting which – with protest
and reproof to the First Cause – I will support
all attempts to bring the human species
nearer its moral senses, and will sign
all protests and appeals for abolition
of warfare from the world, if I can find
where to send them that might have effect.

Failing which, I modestly propose
acceptance of the Curse, but with control.
Allowing violence its primal place
omit the killing, and decide the issues

in a closed place, between professionals
– the framework there and waiting; the result
as meaningful as any carnal chaos.

Or – accepting death – eliminate
the element of waste; sending the leaders,
and all participants in their decisions
and free from body contact until now,
naked against each other in a pit;
granting the victory, and the final right
to arbitrate on all disputed matters,
listed beforehand, to a lone survivor.

I would be even willing to assist
with my own first proposal; arbitrating
in cases of dispute at mortal chess.

Not with the hangings or decapitations
– I hate the sight of blood. A mere injection
leaves me uneasy for a while.

                              Although
if needed, I could offer my assistance
behind the scenes, with the administration:
preparing the site; preparing the instruments;
consoling the victim on the night before.

Even, on the day, as an assistant,
holding something for the celebrant
– viewing the proceedings as a sacrifice.

NOTES

1. An Insect Analogue

Columns of ants, determined and in order,
destroy their own kind.
                                    This is a semblance.

Answering the intermittent call
– nomadic; the mass impulse of the group
centred bloodless in a single will –

they will extinguish with indifference
any interruption in their path.

2. By the Dead Sea

The terrible voice of God
will thunder the truth of His glory
and the hosts of Heaven exclaim
to weaken the base of the world.

Then the rains of Hell will descend
on every part of the earth.
The rivers will flood with fire
so the trees on their banks will burn
from the sources out to the sea.

Tongues of flame will discover
the fault in the world's foundations
and all in the land of the living
at the hour of the final judgement
will wail as they cease to be.

This is the war of Heaven.
Its warriors scourging the world,
fulfilling the doom appointed.
Total. Beyond compare.

from *The Dead Sea Scrolls*:
Hymn Number 10

3. A Sleeping Cancer

A cancer wakens when the human creature
musters together. It sharpens behind a cause;
the cause of no account.

                         The First Crusade
answered the holy call, their pious purpose
focused in the distance on the Cross.

Halting en route to ease their daily cares,
the warriors of Christ found satisfaction
beyond fulfilment of their passing needs

– the taste of vengeance. Drunk on Jewish blood,
they wiped their swords, and crossed the Rhine, renewed,
raping onward toward Jerusalem.

4. The War Horse

And the Lord spoke to Job,
saying out of the whirlwind:

                              '… the horse:
was it you who gave him his strength,
covering his neck with thunder?
Who could frighten him, like a grasshopper?

The glory of his nostrils is terrible.
He gallops in the valley, loving his strength,
laughing at fear. He attacks armies!

He does not avoid weapons: he wears weapons
– a shield, a sharp spear and a lance –
and consumes the ground with rage,

smelling the distant battle.
He says: *Aha!* – hearing the bugles
and hearing the captains' commands and the clamour…'

                    from *The Book of Job*: XXXVIII…XXXIX

5. Instances from the Greek

Two named Ajax fighting side by side
– two eager straining bullocks; red, in sweat.

Men of the first Ajax fought beside him,
to rest him when he tired.
                           Men of the second
settled behind, not relishing close combat;
without the plumed helmets, spears or shields;
believing in slings and bows of the twisted wool.
These warriors from Locris –from the rere –
sent sharp showers across the heroes' heads,
causing great havoc. That was the turning point,
when the Trojans lost their fondness for the fray...

from *The Iliad* XIII. II. 700-725

*

Other Classic history texts survive
recording the use of order to the full
in instigating and conducting wars.

Two nation states contend before a third
whose backing is at issue. Arguing
from actions and reactions in the past,

the auditors retire to judge the merits,
returning with the enemy of choice
in firm commitment. This at the point of cause.

Order maintained further, into process.
As when a pair of coastal states, resolving
at last on conflict, putting out to sea,

would bid their two fleets to form in line
and hoist agreed signals: only then,
when each was sure the other was prepared,

would the ships bear down upon each other,
ranked poles beating the salt surface,
in battle order to the point of contact.

Then the confusion. Multiple collisions.
The sailors leap from ship to ship, transformed
– oars let fall and weapons seized in riot –

coming against each other in the chaos
in various setting and predicaments,
slaughtering each other as they meet.

Action lasting through the hours of light;
slackening in the dusk; ceasing at last
by tired consensus. Then the tidying,

clearing the site, the two sides – by agreement –
collecting their sodden bodies from the tide.
The remaining ships homing among the wreckage.

Groups of prisoners, taken through the day,
put to death – part of the tidying;
the fact recorded without emphasis.

*

There are records, equally complete,
of orderly debate after the battle
between the parties. One with the upper hand,

the other having yielded on certain terms
and finding these uncertain in the event;
a flavour of hysteria in the air.

The issues brought forward for discussion
and negative pronouncement, one by one.
The persons deemed responsible brought out

one by one, in turn, and put to death.

BELIEF AND UNBELIEF

NOVICE

I was out late, by myself,
in the last light near the river;
   beginning to be solitary in my habits.

When a thin insect
appeared on a stone near my foot.
   Fragile, with delicate wings,

but hard and alien up close:
the wings narrow and open down flat
   on a jointed gut pointed back straight;

stick legs angled up off the back
and forward off the neck;
   the black bead eyes staring nowhere.

Exactly the same as in the old animal book
with the big grey pictures
   in the wardrobe in the back bedroom;

the species that eats only while it is growing;
that cannot eat once it has reached maturity.
   Designed for its exact needs.

My senses alive in the night:
the sounds of the broad river
   flowing in the shadows past the end of the field;

a half memory of the smell of clothes
covering the animal book – my name on the first page
   with a date from before I was born;

and a tiny taste of death,
with my foot crackling the insect's little glands
   in the dry moss on the stone.

DELIRIUM

I

Veins still beating
thick in the temples.
Arms and elbows
strapped to the torso.
Pelvis straining
up from the table.

Joints still jerking;
wired to a window
high in the wall;
a distant healer
and masked assistants.

Uproar ended,
Will drained bare
back to the dark
and the depths that I came from.

II

The doctor halted
at the foot of the bed
in his hospital coat.

In his late twenties.
Recently qualified,
to my dazed respect.
Our eyes
feeding on each other.

III

Someone will please get me
out of this place

away from the familiars
nosing around the screen

and passing at my feet,
saying nothing.

Come to see me sick
that would not see me well.

SUPERFRESH

I pulled the trolley to one side,
into the recess with the special bread,
to find the list in one of my pockets
and check the next choices.
The leather overcoat wet and heavy,
my collar raw against my beard from the snow.

A woman stopped in front of me. Her face
thin, her voice sharp.
                            In what have I offended…?
But she was asking, in a thick accent,
where I came from; saying
that she came from Russia.
She stood there, no longer young,
waiting for an answer.

                            I understood;
I told her where I came from
and her eyes faded. She spoke again,
her voice distant, saying something
nondescript and lonely. Our spirits
disengaged, somewhere above the Alps.

In my leather overcoat; in from the Winter;
bearded; not from Russia;
I touched the backs of my fingers

against her cheek, abstract-intimate,
in a fragrance off the shelves
of Italian loaves and French boule.

ECHO

He cleared the thorns
from the broken gate,
and held her hand
through the heart of the wood
to the holy well.

They revealed their names
and told their tales
as they said that they would
on that distant day
when their love began.

And hand in hand
they turned to leave.
When she stopped and whispered
a final secret
down to the water.

ART OBJECT

Her face buried in the live neck,
her top lip pulled back,
the fangs dug deep.
She is aware of nothing
but the immediate need.

Her young prey is aware
of his part, and accepts it
with panic and protest,
but understanding. A need fulfilled.

Born in pain, brought to near perfection
in delicacy and swiftness, his lot
to be selected at random, and stopped.

Later, in the stillness after the completion,
the others will come, moderate
and methodical – and also necessary –
for the remains; to occupy and restore the scene.

BELIEF AND UNBELIEF

Legendary Figures, in Old Age

I saw there a number of elders
in intimate companionship,
their old shapes without shame,

playing with one another
– with all that remained
of the barbed shafts of Love.

And I heard one of them saying
to those around her:
'We cannot renew the Gift

but we can drain it to the last drop.'

Lost Cause

And others, grey-featured and slow-moving,
that were condemned to deal only with the symptoms,
endlessly, to the wasting of their eternity.

And without effect,
                        because they had not
sought the causes of their complaints.

Ceremony

Kneeling before the altar
   under the bowl of blood
   with the seed of living light,

I have yielded to an impulse
   growing in the cold mornings
   as I passed the great blank door;

and entered. Walked in the high darkness
   among the pious presences
   praying before their candles.

And knelt at the marble rail;
   my palms together
   before the hidden Host.

          *

It is accomplished.
   I am considering
   the detail in the cold stone.

My breath warm on my fingers.
   My knees damp and chill.
Awareness of the body.

          *

I will return through the high dark
   among the shadowy believers
   out onto Westland Row
                    into the world.

Foetus of Saint Augustine

It is a while since that dusk, among others,
whey they lay together in pleasure,

mouthing each other's names
with eyes half closed, and sighs and body liquids:

the little shape is bent under her heart,
as though examining the terms offered,

or examining the carnal basis
for issues of such spiritual complexity,

or as if listening for a breath of wind
that has passed, and might return.

Genesis

The beginning might as easily have been set
among the people at the farther boundary,
near the Northern dark. Where the grass,
in their own coarse words, was plenteous enough
to make their herd animals burst…
Swamp dwellers; promiscuous;
users of wicker vessels covered with skins.

Their stories, too, were of exile and dispossession,
family division, fatal women, honour and shame,
rivalry, wrath, alien kings, births foretold or exchanged.
And Fate took shape among them as a great queen,
ravenous and with black wings.

Prayer I

In a disordered and misguided community
it is the accomplished and the more fulfilled
who are to be found to one side,
unwilling to take part.

Dear God, let the minds and hearts
of the main body heal and fulfil
as we will watch for the first sign
of redemption:

                    a turning away
from regard beyond proper merit,
or reward beyond real need,
toward the essence and the source.

Prayer II

That the humours settling
     hard in our heart
may add to the current
     of understanding.

That the rough course
     of the way forward
may keep us alert
     for the while remaining.

Addendum

And remember that My ways
that can seem in the short term
mysterious and unfair
and punishing to the innocent

will justify in the end
the seeker after justice
and not the power seeker
crumpled in his corner.

FAT MASTER

ELDERLY CRAFTSMAN AT HIS BENCH

At my worn workbench, in my bent body,
I am disturbed sometimes by an alien fantasy.
Always the same. The detail distinct:

a soft arm reaching toward me
out of nowhere,
the fingers closing and opening.

I believe now that this is an appeal
from serious efforts, like my own, reaching
unfulfilled from somewhere in the past,

and have learned to put my work to one side;
to relax; to think my way back
into the depths beyond their origin,

and to appeal to their source to call them back.
Tell them there is no peace here.
And comfort them on their return.

This restores a serviceable calm,
so that I can attend to my work again.
Hoping there will be a like thoughtfulness
for me and my concerns when the time comes.

INTO THY HANDS

The theme and its right treatment.

The whole and all its parts
made of a given substance.
The parts self-selected,
tried along the senses,
founded on hard practice.
The whole shaped and corrected
to stand unsupported.

All offered to an intimate,
wayward in acceptance,
self-chosen and unknown.

THE LAST ROUND: AN ALLEGORY

We howled down off our benches
at the two figures leaning on each other's bodies
remote and bare under the lights.
All their skills perfected for this meeting.

*

It is a long while since they were first heard of;
since the scouts were sent out to confirm the rumours,
and the first serious offers were made.

They were confined immediately, far apart;
trained by specialists
and strengthened in bodily endurance.

Their names were made public in due course,
and the first local contests arranged
– unimportant in themselves, but essential
as a first step, and for the experience.

One was sent out to meet a local champion
on the champion's own ground; and floored him,
featuring with startled comment in the neighbourhood paper.

After a like shock,
the other came home to great acclaim
and the sponsoring of parochial events.

*

The bell beat,
and echoed up into the dark spaces around us.
It was over.

The two bodies leaned upon each other,
intimate under the lights.
Their fists hung loose in their leather,
their organs damp in their bags.

They were separated.
The arm of one was elevated.
And the two bruised faces
stared away from each other out at the dark.

THE GUARDIANS

We cleared away the debris from an inner gate
and found a number of ancient dried figures
fallen partly asunder beneath the stale shelves.

Our scholar picked up an inscribed fragment
from among them, saying with satisfaction:
– It is in the old language, and clear.

Peace. We are the guardians.
Chosen from among the many
because we were without immediate value.

SUMMER EVENING: CITY CENTRE

In the last light at the end of the Lane
a faint golden haze shimmered.
A cloud of midges, teeming, minute.

Furious in their generation,
they dance among each other
to keep their places toward night and nothing.
A system of selves consuming itself,
worrying at its own energies;
the outer boundary self-established;
without a centre.

*

There are certain mind-specks active among us,
upsetting their near neighbours,
who seem called upon
to take account of the given conditions
and of their own particular burden.

Inspected closely,
would these have anything beyond themselves
to occupy them in their confusion?

She continued:

'There is an inadequacy and an imbalance
in the source material.
This is the basis of energy.

And there is a dysrhythmia in some among you
– the watchful and the partly fulfilled.
A worrying for evidence of purpose.

This gives no pleasure.
But welcome it if it is offered. Use it
to the full. Trusting there will be

an easing of the disorder at a time to come.
But content…'
She turned away, her voice tired.
                    '…if there is not.'

REFLECTION

Eastward,
> *past Liverpool and across the Alps*
toward thoughts of a Beginning:

Jewel of the Total,
solitary and most high,
radiant in nothing.

Who, toying with matter
and with cause and effect,
discovered disorder and the self.

And Who, trying with these
whatever extremes it was
of conscious indignity that interested You,

found me, solitary
and toying with my own basics
of progress and waste,
until I found

You and Your preoccupations.
And You faded into Your own Self.

I pray You to remember me, as I retire
homeward across a darkening Earth,

still curious at my contaminated conception;
not convinced that my existence
might ever have been of relevance;

and doubtful of any usefulness
in my awareness of my condition;

but thankful, on the whole,
for this ache for even a minimal understanding.

FREE FALL

I was falling helpless in a shower of waste,
reaching my arms out toward the others
falling in disorder everywhere around me.

At the last instant,
approaching the surface,
the fall slowed suddenly,

and we were all
unconcerned,
regarding one another in approval.

FAT MASTER

The clamorous toccata is ended;
the pipes shrilled and bass-blasted clear;
a swarm of living impulses
man-handled and stamped into lasting form.

Stunned on our benches
we have got the first part of what we came for.
Overhead and everywhere around us
the church air is silent
except for the memory of a dead last echo.

Packed pause and the ache of control.

      *

From my place in the dark
I think I can see you.

           Fat Master.
Seated. Facing and embracing your great Machine:
the choir of pipes erect
multiplex above your face.

Your fingers busy again at the banked keys,
your boots on the pedals with power
and the delicate weight of the dance,
the first flights of a new fugue
ascend to fill the holy spaces.

The bass lungs, powered by the hidden bellows,
deliver their prime theme into the vault;

sinews of the treble counter swiftly up,
double-coiling on themselves in the spiral design of life.
A whole system assembles among the rafters.

Vital elements circle the centre
of their consenting selves
in the rhythms of ritual,
each in its place, discovering
new affinities and new awarenesses
in the mathematics at the heart of matter.

And now, obedient to your thumbs and fingers,
the chosen from among them begin their return
into the waves of new matter
you send upward to meet them
in growl of the bass and torque of the treble.
Like discoursing with like

until, the essentials agreed
to your satisfaction, and theirs,
they disengage, grateful in the roar of release,
and complete their return

echoing among the columned dark arches
and among the aisles of shades
on our benches:

some that are breathing around me,
silent in mind; and others,
silent and absent,
that have occupied the same places.

Who know that under your courtly courtesies
– bowing forward with your orderly offering

of new discoveries,
and your decorous bowing back –

anything can happen.
      That your offerings
are to the one adequate reflecting Other.
And that we may accept only what we can

of the positives and the perishables,
raw with the rhythms of the real,
you have directed into the organ-darknesses

multiple-moving at your command;
and relieved of the perishable

to consider themselves,
freed into their lasting forms;

to regard the Master in parting,
with His mark upon them;

and to descend upon us
to where I lift my face in thanks.

LOVE   JOY   PEACE

RESERVED TABLE

We stepped down off the footpath
into the basement area
and were welcomed by our host
into the crowded smoke and the waves of jazz.

He led us to our front table,
toward a few musicians
playing at each other on a low stage.

They grew more elderly as we approached;
but gamy, ready for the long night,
their bald leader jerking his canisters off the beat

at a dark contralto, half bare
and serious in her shiny red shift,
little specks of silver alive all over her body.

She sang low, her left arm thrust out toward us.
Her right fist inserted a black instrument
in at her mouth.

          Through wet full lips
she murmured above our heads about love and blood
as we were settled in our places at her feet.

ANATOMY

The flesh is active,
carrying the self onward
in ignominy and fuss.
    Embodying Process.

The self, concerned primarily
with the business of survival,
and worrying at the flesh,
    discovers Love.

Awareness, to one side,
an accident of flesh and circumstance,
is irritated by their behaviour,
    not discerning Purpose.

A part, passive in process
and studying its own condition,
presumes from inadequate data
    to understand the whole.

COLLOQUY OF THE CARNAL

The self – brain and body –
active in love and blood
is custodian of the First Cause.

Eager in early effort,
determined in trial and error,
persistent in inquiry,

it bears the Source
in its red meat

toward an indistinctly conceived Other
waiting, unbegotten,
at the appointed place.

They will meet once,
speechless,
in carnal understanding.

FLESH EATER

I can feel You
wakening among us again.

Is there anything we might offer You
to lessen the hunger
of the next phase?

The great Mouth
opened out of nowhere;
said: 'Truth'

and swallowed Its own word.

THE NEXT PART OF THE PRAYER

– accepting; but not appreciating

that You should require us
to choose among our most valued ones
for our offering;

and that You should have exacted from Your own Self
the substance of a Son,

> torn between flesh and spirit;
> splayed in shame;
> pale with the weight of Love;

when You might have devised everything
exactly to Your requirements.

TENANTS IN COMMON

A hiss from near my heel.
A slither up out of the shallows.
And my old opposite
breathed out of the branches in my path.

'I had been hoping for this.
To solve our joint requirements:
you, needing my nothingness
to quieten your fevers;
I needing the pulse of life
for my inertia.
We were made for each other.

Misplaced here together,
who knows for how long more;
neither asking to take part;

both hoping for the unexpected
to improve matters;
knowing it is unlikely.

I have decided, therefore,
to make as much of things as I can.'

The thin leathery lips approached my neck.

LOVE   JOY   PEACE

I

Many years ago, in our first neighbourhood,
there was an unknown that no one ever saw,
who left his mark painted everywhere:

LOVE   JOY

PEACE

white inside the white sign of a heart.

On blank walls.
On the big rock under the railway bridge
on our way home;
and the end wall of the terrace
at the last turn into our street.

*

Forgotten for a lifetime.

Remembered lately, when I found myself
at the shelves, uncertain;
checking my understanding
of the beliefs of the first Church

– the living witnesses, the chosen few
sheltering together after the calamity.
Leaderless. With their own first followers.
And their memories of the Christ.

The records differ in detail, but all are agreed
on His nature as a man: compassionate and precise
in His judgment of men's conduct;

arrogant and gentle in fatal combination.
Torn from the flesh in carnal pantomime
– too direct for this world.

Records of the last meal show the early signs
of theatre, as the courtesies formed themselves
under their otherworldly burden
into the first outline of a sacrament.

*

And the generations of believers
succeeded each other, multiplied and dispersed;
leaving a growing waste of ornament
between themselves and the Beginning;
the waste increasing through the centuries
into what had been bothering me
– the hierarchies; councils of elders;
elaborate, self-admiring men
embracing each other, dressed up like old women,
in a frankincense odour of property.
The Temple clattering with worldly goods.

•

A house swept bare by Martin Luther.
The gift of grace confirmed
in love and joy and peace.

For Luther the thought of an Almighty God
judging our violations of the Law's demands,
and fixing our punishments, was unacceptable.
We are saved. By the grace of Christ.

Our good deeds are the fruits of direct faith.
Our consciences set free from guilt, and at peace,
we obey the Law with joyful, creative obedience
and spontaneous love, placed direct in our hearts
by the Holy Spirit, in mercy and forgiveness.

II

Grace.
        In a light cast from the world to come,
the mark of Favour. In our earthly light,
gift of the true decision at every choice,
with the strength to endure trial and resist temptation.

That some will turn toward the light
while others, of equal-seeming merit,
will turn aside toward destructive thought and conduct
was, for Augustine likewise, a matter of grace.

Circumstance plays a part: good family or bad;
nurture and health; good or bad fortune.
But at the defining instant of decision
the human creature, imperfect
and exercising the fleshly appetite,
is redeemed by enabling grace.

The mark of grace is spontaneity;
freedom from that burden
which is itself the mark of original sin.

Spontaneity.
                        As a mark of grace.
That the select only, the chosen few,
should enter effortless into the Kingdom
to meet a Maker wasteful on high
as in his worldly works.
                        Unacceptable.

In the chronicles it would seem as much a mark
of disregard: the slack impulse indulged;
the nod – preoccupied with other matters –
for the deed of blood.

Of grace in art.
                        Divine afflatus:
the stage-Shakespeare, not blotting a single line;
Mozart and his deathless simplicities,
noted down while he conversed; Picasso
baring a woman's body
and her mind smiling in sleep
with a half dozen prehensile lines.
The chosen few.
                        Unacceptable.

I rest my faith in the orders of earthly genius,
the day labourer: Michelangelo
manipulating immensities of mind and matter
into great shapes of monumental might:
Ben Jonson's mortal Beloved
...*that must sweat to write a living line;*
Bach working to the lordly need
– the occasional requirement – daily, methodical,
into the heart of matter.

                    Grace as routine.
The lone artificer loosening the charged facts
from an imagination arguing with itself
until the ache is eased – by the will, in tedium.
And the ache-object eased in its correctness
out of the containing inexactness.

                    •

Grace as desire.
                    Amor of Saint Augustine
brooding in body shapes at the edge of faith.

Joy of the flesh.
                    Saying all it can of love.

Peace and nothingness of the last end.

LAST POEMS

Poems written, revised, and recovered, 2013–2021

I
A light tightness

A tightness in the breathing
and the mind – everything too familiar.
Emptiness finding its way
through the bowels up into the heart.

2
And then we watched the trial

And then we watched the trial,
witnesses in the jury;
Experience: the interlocutor
and Time the accuser
consuming the defence.

And we saw the case lost
though it still drags on
while evidence is obstacle to feeble man.

And the Great Inquisitor
advances in a cold wave,
coming to sweep the law away.

20 Sept 2020

3
Beauty

The pale bare soul
is the heart of a closed flower.
In warmth and conscious tenderness
petal and petal unfolds
thought and thought curls away, and
worm-soft
the soul
(which is life)
is exposed.
In its presence
that which is beautiful
(which is also a closed flower)
opens and exposes its soul.
And its soul is the life of the everlasting spirit
flowing from beyond
through
and beyond all things.

Communion, pure is the sacrament.

26 July 2020

4
Christmas Eve 1950

We have come to the meeting of the ways.
The book is laid aside,
That deep book, an ancient tale,
Of a favoured son of God, Lord of Egypt.
Then, in the ancient days,
The way of a man of God was wide,
And his goal was wide and filled with a light
Which melted the edge of the earth
Which mind made.
And in the light, and of the light,
And the light,
Was the Great God, indefinable.

And Joseph, where that page lies open,
Speaks before Pharaoh,
Cunningly and wisely,
And their two minds search in heaven
And grope in the misty
Equivocal stuff of God.

The coals are fading. My lamp glows;
My book rests open on a couch.
I think of one poet
Whose lamp glowed in a tower,
Who wrote of the herald angel
On Christmas Eve
Through the world's clouds down-steering;
And of another
Whose subtle words
Searched behind the picture
For the dry thought

Drifting on the quick void
Where love and imagination
Colour the dark
Which is the nearest we might get to Truth.

And their labours set me the scene:
The way of ancient man
Who knew the spiritual
And lived in God,
Cowardly and terrified.
That way is closing again
Like rays of light that are like rapiers.

The rays strike,
And shining alone in the darkness
Is the one way,
The way of the timeless God
Who has pierced and entered Time.

Revision of unpublished poem, in Box 3, folder 14 in Emory University,
20 Sept 2020

5
Cold reptile eyes are watching/ In a marble face

In a marble face, beneath a marble forehead.
Cold reptile eyes are watching

Two grey lustreless smooth blind man's eyes
seeing, as the blind see, all times and all things.

6
Communism

An ideal system of government;
Based on goodwill,
A willingness to share.

But not practical, given
The malice and greed of the species.

---

15 Nov 2021

7
On 'Darwin: *Origin of Species* ' (1860 ed.)

Conclusion: "Thus, from the war of nature, from famine and death, the most exalted object which we are capable of conceiving, namely, the production of the higher animals, directly follows. There is grandeur in this view of life, with its several powers, having been originally breathed by the Creator into a few forms or into one; and that, whilst this planet has gone cycling on according to the fixed law of gravity, from so simple a beginning endless forms most beautiful and most wonderful have been, and are being evolved."

A presentation of his findings, verging on prayer: addressed to a Creator, to ward off the possible anger of his time. The double meaning of the secondary image of the planet 'cycling' seems intended.

8
Death in Ilium

Truth deserts the body,
Care and power relax:
Hector among his books
Drops dead in the dust.

The patient shadow-eaters
Approach with tough nose
And pale fang to expose
Fibre, weak flesh, speech organs.

They eat, but cannot eat.
Dog faces in his bowels,
Bitches at his face,
He grows whole and remote.

Recovered version, written during Yeats's Centenary year and performed
on the occasion of the laying of the foundation stone of the Lyric Players
Theatre, Belfast on 12 June 1965

9
Enter Richard, dying (from *Downstream*)

(alternate title, 'String-puppets')

Enter Richard, dying; manipulated
On withering cords; his high shoulders hooked
To an infinitely proceeding heaven. Claws
Audible, a crabwise frittering asunder of strength.

Lamplit by the hell-dark laurel hedge
There stood erect in soiled evening dress
One sombrely displaying a starched breast,
Lionlike hair agleam on a dried skull;
Lifting, with a deadly exhaling smile,
Claws outstretched up to a lighted window.

To his desk, lonely, Richard—a Dying Gaul,
The tie loose about a spongy throat.
His pulverising hands hang at his sides,
His thirsty face jerks up to the chalk light.

Issued for his ninety-third birthday May 2021, limited edition of thirty-five copies produced by Liam Keaveney

10

Fragments – After a Fashion

I

I told you this: told you this thing
Which no one but you could understand,
I told you - I was dead.
You questioned all this, saying
'We passed the house of sadness:

                                 You were sad
Because of the leaves, rain spread upon the steps:
Because of a man who deliberately came,

---

15 Nov 2021

11
I feel an invisible movement around us

(alternate title, 'Terminus')

I feel continuous about me
an invisible dull movement;
the beating of mighty and weakening pulses,
pressure on the tenants of all times
toward

12
Judge of the Supreme Court

There are those
from whom I expect little
in the long term.

But there is always the one:
that formal student,
with thin umbrella.
Quiet, always in on himself,

23 June 2021

13
Luminous in the darkness of the past

Luminous in the darkness of the past
soft surfaces are alive
and quiet;
the smooth planes curve
rising to fullness
and narrowing to silent cupped lips

opening to the vessel of eternity
Fingers caress and bent brow is cooled
forever in a music
of a world beyond this world.

---

23 June 2021

14
Night Elder

I was standing on the top landing
as I often do when retiring,
looking out at the night;

 – when there appeared in mid air before me
a bare baby, male; passing,
little head first.
It turned toward me, as it passed,
an old man's face. And was gone,

I continued to my room
Loneliness in my loins,

23 June 2021

15
Old

Old,
with grasping outstretched arms,
ragged wings.

Angry, fingers,
white flames;
Sting their corpses,
Hunt them to your knives,
Face to Face;

Crop them where they hesitate,
stab their wide eyes;

Pluck down with silver hand
Crush with heel and hand
The serpent's head.
Spill their drained lives,
Its ragged weave.

The dead host distributed
in the roads.

20 May 2021

16
Our Father 2020

Our Father;

         Idle Finger,
stirring nothing into something,
and something into what.

In the half light
fingering my own faults.

31 July 2020

17
Our Father 2021

Our Father

        mighty Finger
that have stirred nothing
into everything that could happen,
I think I can see You at Your solitary recreation,
idling; causing and cancelling;
All-Knowing, but taking Time off;
placing Your pieces for one more start;
All-Knowing, but suspending awareness
or judgement of each outcome;
allowing us each a brief self in our generation.

Let there be Good,
with the slightest deficiency of Bad to maintain movement.
and do not, I beg,
look upon me as I am,
nearing, fingering my own faults.
myself, I must accept
wishing that I could adapt.

18
Our Home

Our Home
Pearl blue and far, small,
small in the dark.
                    A pearl,

I can scarcely believe what goes on there.

19
Reflection of a Poet

Why should you take a pen and hold it so
And stare at twenty ruled lines on a page
Feeling the solid things break up and go
To pieces, and time break adrift from age?

Perhaps you've just been reading and a thought
Stirred by the sentences has taken fire
And burned away the meaning that you bought
And all that's left is this ash-grey desire.

A mental passion, like a painless sore
That vaguely is, and waits for its relief.
You might, to find your poem, try any door,
Housebreaking outward, an upended thief.

You, like a thief, have got a tender tip
That reaches to and shrinks from things around
And you, like he, crouch, fingering a lip
And steal selectively from what you've found.

But what is it to be? There is so much
That here and there a reckless hand has hurled.
Will you with intimate or prouder touch
Settle a mood or make another world?

Take what you like, but count yourself the great
Item of spoil and if you take the way
Joining the world's centre to your fate
You in the mirror will know what to say.

Revision of poem from *National Student* (October 1951)

20
Stars ticked uncontrollably down

Stars ticked uncontrollably down the night face,
registering another million routine stoops
into the kindling reeds
as quietly accomplished again.

At the same hour two lips were seen to break the crests of speech in
fair order.
For reply I find I am left with an unanswerable
dawn upon my hands.

Revision of 'First Light', *Another September*

2 I
Statuesque

Stone knees, hands, cold breasts, stony-eyed,
they are nothing but what they are made;
raised by human hands from a rock side,
lifted out of sleep by the chisel-blade

We are made of stone,
stony-eyed, placed in repose.
Out of the rocks' ribs we were lifted,
out of sleep, out of repose.

into a monumental life, with a sweeping
hold on years that they cannot realise;
with a burrowing hold in stone; no fatal creeping
of change shadowing their stony eyes.

We have been given lives
too long, lasting with stone,
and so our time is almost empty,
except of despair; we accept despair.

These quarried creatures express the unbroken
need of man to utter the speechless, and make
eternal gesture. Impossible to be spoken,
that poignant inclination of the neck…

With forearms weighing into knees
I sit with locked hands
hanging in my body's shadow.
People forget each other
looking in my face
and taste the stirred fragments of their hands.

I almost make it clear
by this dropped posture
that not they alone are moved;
but they are saved
from having to endure
by an obscuring blank

coldly tying their eyes.
They stand vaguely reproved
before the white tower
of our uniting tongues of desire,
At the top this gravid pose
is, with unspeakable stress,

contrived to show in me, graven in grace,
why the marble and granite thousands,
whether stopped in stride, or quiet,
or wound down, spasm bright,
are, as of old use,
all inwardly bowed under despair's abundance.
Pause after pause of faces

pass, moth-white, my isolation
and die in diminution.
Furrow after furrow
their lives pass, their hour reduces.

In a marble face, beneath a marble forehead,
cold reptile eyes are watching
recedes among the statues
sleeping lapping at lonely feet.
Deserted, and washed white,
and my words frozen into my mouth,
I cannot darken our beauties

with speech, although alien waves
of death, scattered and softer
than dying thunder, rise
to a sardonic voice
of inward echoes, grooves
of inextinguishable laughter.

Plunging aloft into an icy night
our stone eyes, facing the cutting teeth
of slow, infinite humour,
suffering, without tremor
in absolute cold, mute,
our poignant inclination is towards death.

Revision of poem from *National Student* (March 1952)

2 2
Street Game for Adults

Find the meanest pair of eyes,
sharp with cunning, short on shame.
Remove the normal human mind;
substitute a swollen self,
oversized but incomplete.

Stand him on the Mortal Mark.

*

Form a circle,
Throw the hatchet.
Run for cover
If he catch it.

Hide and seek.

Close your eyes
and bare your necks.
Say your prayers
and start counting.

18 August 2021

23
Street Noises

Run out! Shake the bells! City,
Stand still! We know it now!
You who are with me, pity
The gaping ones! Tell them how!

Tell them how it happened. Through
The streets, homes, shops, go!
The old thing that came out new
Must be shown. Run out! Show!

You, sir, with your mouth ajar,
And your eyes open. Come here!
Sit down here with me. That car!
Stop it! Driver lean out! Hear!

I met a man last night. He
Showed me this cheque and said…
Please! Quieten the crowd. We
Must try to reach the farthest head.

He said:… 'This sum. Fifteen figures.
Yours for the loveliest thing.' I won it!
I pulled all together a million triggers,
And that was it! We've done it!

My dear sir! You are weeping!

24
The Choice

Drink the blood
of a lifted head,
newly dead,
and swallow both eyes.

Meat

    *

Bite into the flesh of an apple,
clean and sweet,
sweet and wet,
and swallow; refreshed.

Meat

---

15 Nov 2021

25
The Starlit Eye

The breathing sea in Dublin Bay
is broad and dark this end of day.
Under a chill and constant wind
she pours her tenuous waters in
to rearrange with touch and whisper
shells and sand learning to lisp her
sibilant, rolling nom d'amour.

The female creatures whose allure
pointed out this time and place
for my surrender turns her face
smugly upwards, her shining eye on
me, but I regard Orion
spreadeagled at a sharp degree
coldly emerging from the sea.

That spare and frigid frame of stars
and the minute particulars
of this girl's patient, cool intent
are not at one, and scarcely meant
to occupy me both together.

I quickly put the question whether
blood should be put down or the bright
and starlit eye be closed up tight
before the judicial blink of a ship,
before the wind and the waves that slip
slyly up the sand, and the boulders'

dim, conspiratorial shoulders.
Their silence is a deep response
that clears away the doubt at once,
insinuating: why imply
that there is a dichotomy?
Earthly strand and abstract ocean
mingle both in soft commotion;
day still separate from night,
gathers in a fluid light.

Suddenly she beside me seems
the meeting place of various streams
converging in a placid mirror
that reflects my simple error.
After a primeval pause
of caution her first yielding thaws
my taut reserve. Without alarm
the problem folds inside my arm
and is resolved by lips and hand
so that we can both understand.

Night grows around our satisfaction
till we tire. In quiet reaction,
standing apart on the sands, in soft
mood we talk and look aloft
at glittering gravel in the sky
to see Orion striding by
suspended handsome, broad and high.

Recovered, without revision to Dolmen Press pamphlet version, 1952

26
The sun

The sun
accurately calculated
slipped down for the last time
and lit for the last time
the religious lines of Cormac's buildings.
Oak and gold plate and grass alleys darkened:
drinkers' voices faded.
the skirt of a grey robe flickered.
During the night the gods and great men died.

---

20 Sept 2020

27
We are the marrow in the serpent's bone

We are the marrow in the snake's backbone
And the world shrinks to hear the marrow moan.

20 May 2021

28
On *Troilus and Cressida* (IV.iv, ll.109–116)

Cressida. My Lord, Will you be true?

Troilus.   Who? I? Alas, it is my vice, my fault:
                 Whiles others fish with craft for great opinion,
                 I with great truth catch mere simplicity;
                  Whilst some with cunning gild their copper crowns,
                 With truth and plainness I do wear mine bare.
                 Fear not my truth; The moral of my wit
                 Is 'plain and true' – there's all the reach of it.

It is clear that both types are needed
to accept the Gift complete;
with that Godgiven tiny addition
of the positive to pass it on living

Let us proceed,
suffering and shouldering our Waste.

ACKNOWLEDGEMENTS

Thanks to the Kinsella family for their help in assembling this collection, and to scholars Andrew Fitzsimons and Adrienne Leavy for their careful attention to the text, especially of the 'Last Poems' document, whose order this edition preserves.